Watch
WHAT YOU SAY

21 DAYS TO REFRAMING YOUR WORLD WITH YOUR WORDS

YVETTE THOROUGHGOOD

Book Cover Design: Prize Publishing House

Printed by: Prize Publishing House, LLC in the United States of America.

First printing edition 2021.

Prize Publishing House

P.O. Box 9856 Chesapeake, VA 23321

www.PrizePublishingHouse.com

ISBN (Paperback): 978-1-7371829-9-3

ISBN (E-Book): 978-1-7374791-0-9

CONTENTS

DEDICATION

I dedicate this devotional to the memory of my late father, Dr. Yd B. Thoroughgood. He exemplified what is expressed throughout this devotional. He was a faith talker and faith walker. I observed him calling forth things, and they would manifest! He was an encourager who spoke life into countless individuals.

Dad, I hope that somehow you can see this; and it makes you smile.

ACKNOWLEDGMENTS

I first wish to thank God for strengthening me through every experience. None of this would be possible without Him. I honor my mother, Lady Shylene Thoroughgood, and the memory of my Dad, Supt Yd B. Thoroughgood. Thank you for instilling biblical principles from my youth and always encouraging me to excel. I can never repay you for all you've poured into my life. Thank you to my sister DiYan, brother in love, Eugene, and their sons, who have always been a source of encouragement, reminding me to take the limits off. I honor my brother and pastor, Dr. Waddee B. Thoroughgood, and my sister in love/First Lady Nekeysha Thoroughgood and their children. Pastor, I would have never written a devotional had you not tasked me with writing a weekly devotional for my home church, Church Of The Advent. To my goddaughter, Deja Mercer, thank you for your prayers and continuous encouragement. I appreciate my bestie, Minister Youlanda Smith, for every prayer, word of encouragement, and every seed sown into my life. I wish to thank Superintendent J. Elwood Gatlin, Sr. and Lady Chavar Gatlin for your words of wisdom, prayers, support, and every opportunity to minister. Thank you, Co-Pastor Sue Lowe, for your love, prayers, and words of wisdom. They have helped me more than you know.

To everyone who will read this devotional, I thank you for your support; and pray that you will be encouraged along your spiritual journey.

FOREWORD

It was David who wrote in the 90th number of Psalms and the 12th verse, "So teach us to number our days, that we may apply our hearts unto wisdom." What David was asking God was to teach us to make good use of the time that God has given us that we may not only adopt wisdom unto ourselves, but we will operate within its limitless boundaries. Many think that money is our greatest commodity, but in all actuality, our greatest commodity here on earth is time, and more importantly, what we do and create with the time God grants us.

When we leave this earthly vessel, and our loved ones lay us to rest, there will be three items on our tombstone for certain the date we were born, a dash in the middle, and the date we transitioned. I believe the most important factor in that equation is the dash in between because, without words, it covers a wide span of decisions and choices we made in life while blessed with the gift of time. If I could pose a question to you today, my question would be; what will you choose to do with the time you've been allocated?

Will you surround yourself with positive people, affirmations, and spirit-filled conversations, or will you allow the nuances of negativity to imprison you in a life living beneath the standard of a child of God?

With all that's going on in the world, we must equip ourselves with the right thoughts in order to produce the correct conversations that will shape our atmosphere for the better. Please understand that your thoughts determine your attitude, your attitude determines your actions, and your actions determine your outcome. Your words reveal your perception of your predicament, and within them, you'll find your fate and your future. Just imagine the efficacy of God's promises declared over your life daily. How would that change your life for the better? Well, I would like to present the opportunity to you to find out; and you couldn't be in better hands than in the ones that will navigate you through this journey.

My grandfather, Pastor John Thomas Thourogood, used to say, "I love milk, but give it to me in a clean glass,"; and I can say undoubtedly that the woman of God in whom you will be feasting from for the next 21 days is indeed a clean vessel.

Evangelist Yvette Thoroughgood is not only an anointed Evangelist, intercessor, and teacher, but she's my blood sister and best friend. I wouldn't be surprised if some of this book stemmed from the moments of encouragement she's shared with me in my times of despair.

Child of God, get ready to change your life through the words you speak because they have the power to kill you or heal you.

Dr. Waddee B. Thoroughgood

Senior Pastor – Church of the Advent and The New Jerusalem COGIC

INTRODUCTION

A well-known furniture store decided to conduct an experiment on plants. There were two plants placed ten feet apart. For thirty days, a group of students praised and complimented one plant, while the second group of students hurled insults at the other plant. At the end of the thirty days, the plant that was praised flourished beautifully. The plant that was insulted drooped terribly. The point of the experiment is that words matter! If plants that lack soul or spirit react in this matter, how much more do our words frame our worlds?

This devotional was birthed out of my own life experience. A few years ago, I went through a very rough period and became extremely overwhelmed. I had to fight anxiety daily due to back-to-back stressful events.

One day it was as though the Holy Spirit awakened my ears, and I started to pay attention to what I was saying. I also began to pay closer attention to what people spoke over me, even if in jest.

I started a journey to improve what I spoke, and over time, I watched my life change for the better. Doors and opportunities that had been closed to me for years began to open. I started feeling and even looking better.

"Watch What You Say" has a two-fold meaning. First, pay closer attention to what you say. The second fold is: "Watch the things you speak come to pass."

I am not implying that no action is needed with your words, but the more you declare a thing, the more likely you will act on it.

Take a twenty-one-day journey with me through the Word of God.

I hope that you will apply the principles outlined in this book and watch your life change for the better.

*"**Repetitive complaining** will attract things for you to complain about.*

***Repeated gratitude** will attract things for you to be thankful about."*

Author Unknown

DAY 1

THE POWER OF THE TONGUE

"Death and life are in the power of the tongue: and they that love it shall eat the fruit thereof." – Proverbs 18:21 (KJV)

Did you know that you prophesy every day? I can hear some of you saying, "But I'm not a prophet." *(Did you say it?)*

The Hebrew word for prophecy is navi', which means "to proclaim, mention, call, summon." Are you prophesying your funeral or your future?

What fruit has been produced as a result of the seeds your tongue has sown?

Affirmation: *My present circumstance is not my outcome. The fact that I have a pulse proves there is more. I will live to see and enjoy the promises of God.*

Homework: Evaluate what you've been speaking for the past few days. Have the majority of your conversations or self-talk had a positive or negative connotation? If your speech has been primarily negative, what will you do this week to change that?

Notes:

_____

_____

DAY 2

DIVINE ASSISTANCE

"Set a watch, O LORD, before my mouth; keep the door of my lips." – Psalm 141:3 (KJV)

Sometimes we need to enlist divine assistance in helping to guard against speaking harshly about ourselves and others. Our words can be destructive, and once said, they're not easily taken back. We have all been guilty of speaking the wrong things. Ask the Holy Spirit for help. Request that He fills your heart and mouth with good things. Sometimes our lips need security.

Affirmation: *Today, I will guard my thoughts and govern my words. I will not speak negatively but will only speak that which edifies. I thank God for the gift of expression through speech. I will not misuse it.*

Homework: Be intentional today. Take a few moments to talk to God about your word life. Ask Him to help you to think about the right things so that you may speak what is right and true.

Notes:

_____

_____

_____

_____

_____

_____

_____

_____

_____

_____

_____

_____

_____

_____

_____

_____

_____

_____

DAY 3

USE YOUR PROPHETIC AUTHORITY

" And Elijah the Tishbite, of the inhabitants of Gilead, said to Ahab, "As the LORD God of Israel lives, before whom I stand, there shall not be dew nor rain these years, except at my word." –
1 Kings 17:1 (NKJV)

Elijah was filled with righteous indignation. He grew tired of the adamant worship of the idol god Baal and all the wickedness that took place under the kingship of Ahab. Elijah used his God-given prophetic authority to decree a thing, a MAJOR thing. It was so major that there was no dew or rain for 3 ½ years. Note that he didn't use a word curse nor do anything to bring attention to himself. Ultimately this drought, and eventually, the rain, gave glory to God. This authority was not exclusive to Elijah. You, too (yes, you, my sister, or my brother), have this same authority. Start decreeing and declaring out of a pure heart and watch God change your circumstance.

Affirmation: *I have prophetic authority. By faith, I will decree a thing and watch it manifest.*

Homework: Start a journal of your decrees. Pray over it. Once you see your decree manifest, go to that page and write DONE. Then give God an incredible praise!

Notes:

_____

_____

_____

_____

_____

_____

_____

_____

_____

_____

_____

_____

_____

_____

_____

_____

_____

_____

DAY 4

CALLING DEAD THINGS BACK TO LIFE

"(as it is written, 'I have made you a father of many nations') in the presence of Him whom he believed – God, who gives life to the dead and calls those things which do not exist as though they did..." – Romans 4:17 (NKJV)

We have often heard that "All we need is for God to speak, and it is settled." While this is true, God has made us in His image and has given us power and authority to decree and declare. If what we speak lines up with the will of God, He will bring it to pass. As stated in the above Scripture, God "gives life to the dead and calls things into existence." Use your faith to speak over the things in your life that seem dead. The dreams, the invention, the business plan, that book that you've stopped writing – use your God-given power to revive them! After this, get to work. Speak what you want to see, and believe God to bring it to pass.

Affirmation: *I am made in God's image, and He has given me creative power. Today I align my words with God's will, and the things I speak will come to pass at the appointed time.*

Homework: Write out a list of dreams and aspirations that seem dead or far gone, then write a specific declaration of life over each of them in a separate column.

Notes:

_____

_____

_____

_____

_____

_____

_____

_____

_____

_____

_____

_____

_____

DAY 5

TIMING IS EVERYTHING

"A word fitly spoken is like apples of gold in pictures of silver." –
Proverbs 25:11 (KJV)

A word spoken at the right time is as precious to the soul as the view of golden fruit in a basket of silver is to the eyes. We have to realize the importance of saying things at the right time and also speaking to others in a way by which the message will be received. We must be intentional about speaking the truth in love. We must consciously decide that we will use our words to edify (*build others up*) and not tear down. My grandmother used to say you can win more bees with honey than vinegar.

Remain prayerful about how you speak to others. Timing is everything.

Affirmation: *I will be careful about when and how I speak to others. My words will edify and not tear down. The law of kindness will be upon my tongue.*

Homework: Encourage three people today.

Notes:

_____

_____

_____

DAY 6

WORDS THAT REFRESH

"As the cold of snow in the time of harvest, so is a faithful messenger to them that send him: for he refresheth the soul of his masters." – Proverbs 25:13 (KJV)

The snow in this verse does not refer to falling snow. Snow from the mountains was used to cool drinks in this context. Imagine working outside on a hot day, and someone brings you a snow cone in your favorite flavor. Refreshing just thinking about it, right? The faithful messenger is refreshing, as he can be trusted to communicate clearly and bring important messages. It is a blessing when your voice is deemed consistent and can be trusted. Not only should we be consistent, but as faithful messengers, our words should be "faith-filled." Do your friends hit "ignore" when you call? Do you have a reputation of leaving others feeling drained after a conversation with you? If you answered yes, it's time to change your perspective and your conversation. Be the snow cone on a hot summer day to all whom you come in contact with.

Affirmation: *My conversation is faith-filled and refreshes the listener.*

Homework: Be conscious of how your listeners feel once you have ended a conversation today. Even if you discuss challenging things, be intentional about speaking the solution and ending on a positive note.

Notes:

_____

_____

_____

_____

_____

_____

_____

_____

_____

_____

_____

_____

_____

DAY 7

KEEP YOUR PROMISES

"Whoso boasteth himself of a false gift is like clouds and wind without rain." – Proverbs 25:14 (KJV)

We must not raise people's expectations with no intention of making good on the promise. In other words, be true to your word or don't say anything. Don't develop a reputation of being "all talk and no action." We must be credible and accountable in our dealings. Your words carry weight; don't waste them just to impress.

Affirmation: *I am a person of my word. I am not a promise-breaker but a promise keeper. I will not set unrealistic expectations. I will be honest with myself and others about what I can and cannot do. I will not boast in an ability I don't have to be viewed as impressive.*

Homework: Make a promise to yourself between you and God and write it down.

Notes:

_____

_____

_____

_____

_____

_____

_____

_____

_____

_____

_____

_____

_____

_____

_____

_____

_____

_____

DAY 8

SPEAK THE TRUTH AND NOTHING BUT THE TRUTH

"A man that beareth false witness against his neighbor is a maul, and a sword, and a sharp arrow." – Proverbs 25:18 (KJV)

A person who tells lies on his neighbor is like a hammer that beats one down to the ground with words. Cruel words are like a sword that attempts to destroy a person's character. "Sticks and stones may break my bones, but words will never hurt me" – one of the biggest lies ever told.

Let's not use our tongues to destroy anyone's reputation.

As a matter of fact, just stop lying! Most lies are rooted in fear and jealousy. Before you spread rumors about your neighbor, expose that part of yourself to God that desires to tear others down. Get to the root of it and be healed. Wounded individuals wound others. This is not God's will for your life.

Affirmation: *I will speak the truth and will not spread rumors about my neighbor. If my words do not help a situation, I will not say anything at all.*

Homework: (For your eyes only) Reflect on the following questions. Do you tend to lie on others? Do you receive gratification from tearing others down? If the answer is yes, what is at the root of this character flaw? Does it make you feel that you have the "upper hand"? Was it done to you? Have you prayed about it? Have you sought counsel?

Notes:

_____

_____

_____

_____

_____

_____

_____

_____

_____

_____

_____

_____

DAY 9

YOUR WORDS CREATE WORLDS

"Through faith we understand that the worlds were framed by the word of God, so that things which are seen were not made of things which do appear." – Hebrews 11:3 (KJV)

You can literally frame your world with your words. When God said, "Let there be...", whatever came after the "be" manifested. He spoke it, and it happened. If you speak negatively, expect to live in a negative world. I remember hearing a true story of a gentleman who repeatedly said, "My back is killing me." He confessed this for days. Within a week, this young man died, and the condition was somehow related to the pain in his spine.

I also know individuals who had life-threatening illnesses speak life over themselves repeatedly; a few of them outlived the doctors that gave them the poor prognosis. If you speak the promises of God, expect the promises of God to manifest.

You have so much untapped power and potential right within your tongue. Don't use it as a weapon; use it to call forth wonders!

Affirmation: *I will reframe my world by faith and the Word of God. I will speak what I desire to see until I actually see it.*

Homework: Take inventory of the spontaneous words you speak over yourself today. Are they aligned with the Word of God and what you really want to see?

Notes:

_____

_____

_____

_____

_____

_____

_____

_____

_____

_____

_____

_____

_____

DAY 10

USE YOUR CREATIVE POWER

"And God said, 'Let there be light,' and there was light." –
Genesis 1:3 (KJV)

I can recall describing the kind of job I wanted, including the salary, during my prayer time. That particular position did not exist at the time. Within a few weeks of decreeing that I would have this role, I received a message that the company I worked for was creating this position and needed four applicants. I applied for this job and knew before the interview was over that the job was mine. Two days later, I was offered the position.

I used my God-given creative power to speak that position into existence. When I accepted the job, nothing was lacking.

When God said, "Let there be light," there wasn't a doubt that the light would come.

God has given us this authority. Activate it! Now, make sure that what you are speaking is aligned with God's will. Speak it and prepare for what you decreed.

Affirmation: *God has given me creative power. I will decree and declare a thing by faith and watch it manifest.*

Homework: Sit with God and reflect on areas of your life where there is untapped potential. What can you create with Him?

Notes:

_____

_____

_____

_____

_____

_____

_____

_____

_____

_____

_____

_____

_____

DAY 11

SPEAK A WORD IN SEASON

"The Lord GOD hath given me the tongue of the learned, that I should know how to speak a word in season to him that is weary: he wakeneth morning by morning, he wakeneth mine ear to hear as the learned." – Isaiah 50:4 (KJV)

If we avail ourselves to hear God's voice, He will educate us on what to say and how to say it. We are living in unprecedented times. People have grown weary and need hope. We never want to miss an opportunity to minister hope and healing, and therefore must be willing to receive instruction from the Holy Spirit. This is not a one-time occurrence. "Morning by morning, he awakens our ears to hear as the learned." Be open and be available for God's use.

Affirmation: *I yield my ear and mind to the Holy Spirit for instruction on how I should minister to the weary. I declare that I have the tongue of the learned and am sensitive to whom I am assigned.*

Homework: Take time in the morning to ask God who you should minister to and what He is assigning you to do for that day.

Notes:

_____

_____

DAY 12

SPEAK WELL OF OTHERS

"Keep thy tongue from speaking evil, and thy lips from speaking guile." – Psalm 34:13 (KJV)

I'm sure when you were growing up, at least one adult said, "If you don't have anything nice to say, don't say anything at all." So much trouble would be avoided if this advice was carried into adulthood. If it's not kind, don't speak it. If it's deceitful, don't speak it. If there is a compulsion to speak evil and deceit, there is a lack of love.

Affirmation: *I will not speak evil of my neighbor, even if I believe my words to be true. I will not be deceitful in my speech. I will speak the truth. I will speak words that build up.*

Homework: Think of one person you have spoken ill of and release the opposite over them in prayer.

Notes:

_____

_____

_____

_____

Yvette Thoroughgood

_____

_____

_____

_____

_____

_____

_____

_____

_____

_____

_____

_____

_____

_____

DAY 13

MIND YOUR MOTIVES

"If any man among you seem to be religious, and brideleth not his tongue, but deceiveth his own heart, this man's religion is in vain." – James 1:26 (KJV)

Religious in this context denotes one who is pure and looks out for the fatherless and the widows. If this is your claim, then you should have control over your tongue. If your speech is reckless, you are deceiving yourself and have an empty religion. There is a way of saying everything. We should also mind our motives for saying a thing. Hurtful speech and speaking at the wrong time only yield ruined relationships and even a loss of life.

Affirmation: *I will be careful to keep my heart pure, as my words are a direct reflection of what I hold in my heart.*

Homework: Ask God if there are areas where your religion has become empty. It's time for a fresh heart and motive check!

Notes:

_____

_____

_____

_____

DAY 14

DECREE AND SEE!

"Thou shalt also decree a thing, and it shall be established unto thee: and the light shall shine upon thy ways." – *Job 22:28 (KJV)*

Say what you need, or even what you desire, and mean what you say. Once you speak with belief, it is established. I can recall years ago going into a store with my mom and sister. I saw a lovely gown that I wanted. Before going into the store, I decreed that the max I would spend would be $25.00. They chuckled. When I picked up the gown, it was more than $25.00. I don't know why I did it, but I took it to the register anyway. By the time numerous discounts were applied, I paid 25.00 for this amazing gown which was worth far more. I still have it to this day and see this gown as a testimony. That may seem minor, but if God honored the words of my desire, how much more would He honor my need? God will not deny you; it is His good pleasure to bless you. God's light will shine upon your ways – He will bless whatever you put your hands to.

Affirmation: *I will decree a thing and believe that it is God's good pleasure to bless me. I will not be denied because my Heavenly Father rules everything.*

Homework: Make a note of the things you really want to see established in this season.

Notes:

_____

_____

_____

_____

_____

_____

_____

_____

_____

_____

_____

_____

_____

Day 15

Moving Mountains

"For verily I say unto you, That whosoever shall say unto this mountain, Be thou removed, and be thou cast into the sea; and shall not doubt in his heart, but shall believe that those things which he saith shall come to pass; he shall have whatsoever he saith." – Mark 11:23 (KJV)

"This mountain" could represent many things. I don't know what you're facing today. It could be debt, sickness, family issues, unbelief, and the list goes on. Speak the solution. Know that God will do it just as well as you know your name. Do not doubt in your heart. Remember that it's not up to us to decide how God will do it. He has that handled. God is waiting on you to do your part.

Affirmation: *I believe, and therefore I will align my language and faith to reflect Mark 11:23.*

Homework: Ask God if there is an area where you need to release worry as you do your part!

Notes:

_____

_____

_____

_____

DAY 16

SPEAK LIFE!

"Then Jezebel sent a messenger unto Elijah, saying, 'So let the gods do to me, and more also, if I make not thy life as the life of one of them by tomorrow about this time." – 1 Kings 19:2 (KJV)

Elijah was the prophet who declared that there would be no dew or rain. He grew tired of the ways of the wicked king and worship of idol gods. Elijah is the same prophet who slew 850 prophets of Baal and Ashera as they were killing the prophets of God. When the wicked queen Jezebel discovered this, she sent word that she would do the same to him as he had done to the prophets. She was mad, and she wanted him dead. In essence, she spoke a word curse.

What is a word curse? A word curse is when someone verbalizes the plan that the enemy has for your life. We are covered by the shadow of almighty God, so we have the power to ward off these types of attacks. However, when we are tired or have grown weary due to life's circumstances, we become vulnerable. While the enemy will not get the advantage, we can sometimes feel the effects of what was spoken. As powerful as Elijah was, he had been fighting and was tired. When he heard the message sent by Jezebel, he hid. Ultimately, her words fell to the ground, and she died a horrible death. Be careful of speaking negativity over a person's life and future. You just may be sending a word curse, which is not of God. You are tapping into another spirit (I will address this in my next book ☺). Even if someone has done you wrong, stop your evil speaking and let God handle it!

Affirmation: *I will not speak death over my neighbor. I will only speak life and that which edifies. I do not receive any word curse spoken over me or my family. I am covered and shielded by almighty God. Nothing by any means will hurt me.*

Homework: Spend some intentional time breaking agreement with any word curses spoken over you that you are aware of.

Notes:

_____

_____

_____

_____

_____

_____

_____

_____

DAY 17

LOVE IS THE KEY

"Though I speak with the tongues of men and of angels but have not love, I have become sounding brass or a clanging cymbal." – *1 Corinthians 13:1 (NKJV)*

We can have the ability to speak multiple languages, including angelic speech. However, if we don't have love, it's equivalent to the sound of clashing metal. Don't become caught up in the gift; make sure it is anchored in love. One day all earthly things will pass away, but love is eternal.

Affirmation: *I will not become consumed with my gifts and abilities, but I will make sure that all I do is anchored in love.*

Homework: Find an area of your personal life where you can intentionally let love in.

Notes:

_____

_____

_____

_____

_____

DAY 18

PURE SPEECH

"Praise and curses come from the same mouth. My brothers and sisters, this should not happen! Do clean and polluted water flow out of the same spring?" – James 3:10-11 (GWT)

It isn't profitable to praise God with the same tongue with which we curse our neighbor. The tongue that blesses God should help instead of hurt. This would be comparable to a tree producing two types of fruit. Unless genetically modified, this shouldn't be possible. God not only hears what we say, but He weighs the heart. Let's keep our minds and our spirits pure so that unpolluted water flows when we speak.

Affirmation: *My speech is aligned with God's will and His way. I will praise God and bless my brother and sister with the same tongue. I am a reservoir of pure, refreshing water to all whom I come in contact.*

Homework: Reflect on not just your words but the thoughts they stem from. Is there a mixture of positive and negative? Pray about re-aligning with God's perspective on whatever the matter is.

Notes:

_____

_____

DAY 19

BE THE EXAMPLE

"Do not answer a fool according to his folly, or you will also be like him." – Proverbs 26:4 (KJV)

It's okay to answer a foolish person, but do not get into an argument with him. Otherwise, you may be labeled as he is. We don't have to lend our voice to every matter. It's okay to be silent. It's perfectly fine to keep your opinion to yourself if it will not improve the situation. Guard your peace and reputation. You never know, the one who is deemed foolish may learn a thing or two from your example.

Affirmation: *I will not become entangled with foolish conversation. If it profits nothing, I will say nothing. I will maintain my peace and reputation.*

Homework: Reflect on what it means to guard your peace today. Are you tempted to engage in battles that are not worth fighting? Release them to God and look to His example so that you can become an example to others.

Notes:

_____

_____

_____

Day 20

Heart Check

"But the things that proceed out of the mouth come from the heart, and those defile the man." – Matthew 15:18 (KJV)

The heart mentioned in this verse is not the organ that pumps blood but rather the source of our motives. What we carry in our hearts takes root in our minds. What we meditate on will proceed from our mouths. If our words and thoughts are corrupt, eventually, our actions will also be.

Affirmation: *I will maintain a pure heart, so my thoughts and speech will honor God and edify others.*

Homework: Let's have a heart check. Have I forgiven? Do I envy others? Do I rejoice in the failure of others? If the answer is yes to any of these questions, pray with me:

"Lord Jesus, please forgive me. Please cleanse my heart, mind, and motives. I really desire to live for You. I want to please You in all of my ways. Please minister to the deepest parts of me. I receive Your love, forgiveness, and healing, in Jesus's name, amen."

Notes:

_____

_____

_____

Day 21

Go Forth and Prosper!

"Beloved, I pray that in all respects you may prosper and be in good health, just as your soul prospers." – 3 John 1:2 (NASB)

You've made it to the finish line! Yay! The above Scripture is my prayer for you. I pray that you are blessed with excellent health and prosperity. I pray that God strengthens you to do all that He has called you to do.

Affirmation: *I decree and declare that I am complete and whole, lacking nothing, from the crown of my head to the soles of my feet. God satisfies me with long life.*

Homework: Decree a blessing over at least five people today!

Notes:

_____

_____

_____

_____

_____

_____

CONCLUSION

Thank you for taking this journey with me. I pray that you will begin to see positive changes in every area of your life. Declare it by faith and reframe your world.

CPSIA information can be obtained
at www.ICGtesting.com
Printed in the USA
BVHW032149080921
616424BV00006B/113